LOOM KNITTING FOR BEGINNERS

INSPIRING METHODS AND
TECHNIQUES FOR BEGINNERS.
CREATING AMAZING ARTWORKS
USING SIMPLE AND EASY WAYS.
LEARN THE BASICS OF LOOM
KNITTING

PATRICIA WILLIAMS

1

Table of Contents

CHAPTER ONE

INTRODUCTION

Loom knitting is the craft technique of the usage of a loom as opposed to needles to create stunning knitted fabric, which may be transformed into sublime homeware, fashions and cosy accessories. While the use of a loom would possibly appearance fiddly commercial enterprise, loom knitting is notably clean when you understand how, and is even exquisite for children!

Learning the fundamentals of loom knitting is an clean manner to get started. With only some simple steps you could ee the knitted fabric forming. Knitting on a loom can produce the same forms of projects that traditional knitting can, along with tricky designs like cables. The advantage to creating those on a loom is that it is often simpler on your palms and it usually works up quicker.

Loom knitting has been around for hundreds, maybe lots, of years. The most dependable data dates returned to the 16th century, whilst someone was looking to create an opportunity method of knitting and framed knitting "machine" became born. If you've ever attempted finger knitting or spool knitting, you'll see the relationship, which may additionally even be how this large form of knitting on a loom got here to be.

The iconic 'loom', which clearly refers back to the cunning contraption used to weave together yarn (or thread) to provide fabric, has great origins from Europe inside the Middle Ages to the complicated craftwork of the Amerindian tribes of the Americas.

Today, loom knitting remains a celebrated method that can be used to create whatever from appropriate wall hangings, hats, scarfs, blankets and beyond!

Loom knitting is particularly super for folks that revel in sore arms, inclusive of those with arthritis or carpal tunnel syndrome. It's also a extraordinary alternative for folks that actually favour a needleless method to their tasks, now not to say that the technique is relatively fast so you can whip up marvellous creations in file time. With a diffusion of knitting looms and a vast spectrum of strategies available, loom knitting offers the premise to create diverse and showstopping initiatives.

CHAPTER TWO

TYPES OF KNITTING LOOMS

Knitting looms are available in different shapes, sizes, and substances, and cross by using an expansion of names such as a knitting board, rake, frame, or the classic loom. Some have a hard and fast number of pegs, at the same time as others are adjustable. You can even make your own!

Just as knitting needles are available one-of-a-kind

thicknesses, which determine the size or gauge of your knitting, the peg length and spacing on knitting looms also determine the gauge. Larger pegs spaced farther apart make cumbersome or open knitting, at the same time as thinner pegs spaced more closely bring about finer or tighter knitting.

Each peg on a loom holds one stitch, so the quantity of pegs also makes a difference. You don't must use each peg for a project, but you do need to have enough to acquire the dimensions of the knitted piece you want. For example, to make a blanket without joining numerous pieces collectively, you'll need many pegs, which you discover on looms fashioned like a massive S. Because the loom length and shape is so important to the outcome of the knitting, it's vital to check that you have the correct loom for a task. Patterns usually tell what form of loom to apply, alongside peg count number and spacing. It's additionally crucial to pay attention to the yarn weight endorsed for a pattern or loom, inclusive of whether to keep a couple of strand of yarn together.

CHOOSING YOUR KNITTING LOOM

There are many varieties of loom to be had depending of the undertaking you're embarking on. While rake (long) looms are amazing for flat panel projects including blankets, circular looms are joyously well suited with hats and cowls. Here are a number of the kinds of loom you're likely to stumble upon in your loom knitting journey!

RAKE LOOMS

Rake looms, also known as lengthy looms, are characterized by a unmarried row of pegs, normally used to create flat panel initiatives which includes blankets and scarves from unmarried knitting. When rakes are set aside each other you then have what as called a knitting board. Some rake looms in the marketplace may additionally consist of two rows with an extra peg on both give up of the loom permitting you to work in the spherical if you so want. Just like regular knitting, cloth created from a simple rake loom may have a knit facet and purl aspect. The gauge of the lengthy knitting loom is decided by means of the distance among each pin, so the closer collectively your pins the finer your knitted cloth!

CIRCULAR AND OTHER ROUND LOOMS

Round knitting looms consult with a loom where there's no preventing factor, not like its cousin the rake. A spherical knitting loom is any tool where you can constantly weave, this could seem in a menagerie of exceptional sizes and styles, which includes circular, oval, square, triangular or even heart-fashioned looms. Round loom knitting initiatives are often (however not completely) tubular shaped due to capability to continuously knit inside the round, this means that in case you're trying to make socks, sleeves or cowls, or anything that could have a tube or circle form - spherical looms are a must!

AFGHAN LOOMS

S-loom, or the serenity loom, has an 'infinity' parent of 8 structure, and is the best knitting loom for crafting massive panels of material which may be sewn together to create dreamy afghans and blankets.

SOCK LOOMS

Sock looms encompass an adjustable gauge so that you can without problems create increases and decreases to knit the best length in your entire circle of relatives, whether you're creating grown up socks or baby booties.

CHAPTER FOUR

HOW TO LOOM KNIT

Your favored knitting stitches can be created to your loom consistent with the way you wrap the yarn around the pegs. Different wrapping techniques will produce specific textures and designs to produce satisfyingly plush tasks from conventional stitches to more problematic patterns inclusive of lace or cable work. Anything is viable with a loom and a bit expertise!

It's crucial to undergo in thoughts often loom knitting stitches have special names to the ones created by way of needles.

HOW TO USE A KNITTING LOOM

Knitting looms are available in a ramification of sizes and styles depending on what type of venture you're making. While lengthy looms paintings first-rate for projects like scarves, spherical (or round) looms are great for hats, socks or something that has a tube structure.

Base, pegs and gauge

Let's get all the way down to basics. The anatomy of a loom is made from three vital additives; base, pegs and gauge. The base is the body at the bottom of your loom which is probably a long or spherical to be had in plenty of sizes. The pegs describe the multiple quick pins connected to the bottom - now and again these are just known as pins. The gauge is the gap between each peg (or pin), the broader the distance is between the pegs the greater the gauge. Easy-peasy!

Row vs peg be counted

When it involves the wide variety of rows and pegs to your loom knitting mission, it's important to take into account that those are not interchangeable. The peg be counted determines the circumference or width of your challenge, and the quantity of rows is how generally you repeat this. If you are making a tubular venture which include socks or a hat on a round loom, then the rows will handiest add to the period of the tube, but now not supply anymore supply across the foot or head.

In addition on your loom and yarn you may additionally need a hook to catch and pull your loops of yarn over to create the knitted stitches.

LOOM KNITTING STITCHES

Just like knitting with needles, loom knitting includes a whole encyclopedia of stitches to craft fantastically textured knitwear.

Before we get to precise stitches, there are essential strategies of knitting on a loom: single and double knitting.

SINGLE KNITTING

Single-knitting is when you knit stitches on pegs next to each other, growing a material a good way to have a 'proper' and 'wrong' facet.

KNIT SEW (OK)

The knit sew on a loom has the very same texture and look as a knit sew created the use of everyday needles. The knit sew is achieved by using your hook to drag at the yarn looped around your peg, to create a new loop. By lifting the old loop up and over, you update with the brand new loop in your peg to create a new knit sew. And that's it!

This is the primal stitch that after mastered may be mixed with purl to create garter sew or maybe ribbed stitches.

FLAT STITCH (F)

Flat stitch is a close cousin of knit stitch, except it's tighter extra compact. Stretch the working yarn throughout the pinnacle loop of the peg and virtually use your hook to boost the lowest loop over and stale your peg, securing the operating yarn in area by using making it a brand new loop.

CHAPTER FOUR

OTHER LOOM KNITTING STITCHES AND HOW THEY WORK

PURL SEW (P)

Just like in conventional knitting, the purl stitch is the opposite of the knit stitch, meaning that the backside of your fabric could be knit cloth the frontside can be purl. Both knit and purl stitches are terrific starting points to launch you into a global of glorious textures and designs as you discover ways to loom knit.

DOUBLE KNITTING

Double-knitting is while you knit throughout rails, if you are the use of a long loom, so you have a front and a back peg, that means you get the equal texture on each aspects of your material.

NO WRAP SEW (NW)

In loom knitting this might be referred to as a flat (stockinette) sew, and while knitting with needles this is called the fundamental knit stitch (k). Just like the fantastic primary cloth produced while knitting with needles, the no wrap stitch creates robust yet superbly adaptable material which can be converted into terrifi accessories and homeware. As one of the maximum simple stitches, the no wrap sew is a staple for the avid loom knitter and can be used on a long loom or spherical one. And that's a wrap!

EWRAP (EW)

Better called the twisted stockinette stitch whilst knitting with needles (tw St st), the ewrap works a treat on both lengthy and round looms.

SINGLE RIBBED SEW OR RIBBING SEW (RIB)

Perfect for gloves and clothes with the enduring ribbed effect, the unmarried ribbed stitch sees ewrap stitches trade with purl stitches on every row developing glorious ridges of yarn.

HOW KNITTING LOOMS WORK

Most loom knitting falls into 3 classes: circular knitting, which bureaucracy a tube; unmarried knitting, which forms a unmarried panel; and double knitting, which forms a reversible, greater thick material. Different types of looms help make this feasible.

You can do unmarried knitting on any sort of loom, at the same time as circular knitting requires a continuous ring or body of pegs. If you've got a round loom however want to make a flat (non-tube) piece of knitting, honestly paintings backward and forward at the pegs rather than going round in a circle.

Both single and round knitting generally begin with an e-wrap forged on, which wraps the yarn around each peg you are using to your project. The process of wrapping stays the same as you upload more rows or rounds of stitches.

Long looms with double rows of pegs are for double knitting. (Some have a peg at each end so you can use them for round knitting, and you could additionally continually use those for single knitting.) Double knitting starts off evolved with a determine 8 forged-on, wrapping the yarn from side to side throughout the rows of pegs, which keeps as you knit.

When doing unmarried and double knitting, you can adjust the size of your venture by way of running on best one portion of the loom. That's harder to do with circular knitting, which wishes calmly spaced pegs for all the stitches.

After wrapping yarn as soon as around all of the pegs, it is time to wrap it a 2nd time. Next, use a knitting hook (which comes with most looms) to boost the lowest loop of yarn up and over the peg, leaving the top loop in location. This completes a knit stitch. After lifting all of the bottom loops over the pegs, you begin once more, wrapping the pegs and making new stitches.

You can also discover ways to make other types of stitches along with conventional purl stitches, loom-knitting-special stitches, and cast-on and bind-off methods to craft styles and shapes for your work.

LOOM KNITTING PROJECTS

1.   Loom knitting hats

2.   Loom knitting scarves

3.   Loom knitting blankets

4.   Loom knitting socks

THANK YOU.

Made in the USA
Monee, IL
05 April 2022